A Glowing Ember of Courage

Ponderings, Poetry and Prayers

Denise Pyles

A Glowing Ember of Courage
Ponderings, Poetry and Prayers

Copyright © 2009 by Denise Pyles

All rights reserved. No part of this book may be reproduced or transmitted in any form or by any means without written permission from the author.

ISBN 978-0-9843474-1-4

Printed in USA by 48HrBooks (www.48HrBooks.com)

For my Anam Cara

Mary K. Moore

Table of Contents

Prayer for a Dawning Hope 9
God the Faithful One 10
The Recession of Worry That Won't Go Away 11
In the Image and Likeness 12
A Sacred Moment of Letting Go 13
The Longing Ache of God 14
A Rainbow of Silence 15
Prayer of Attentiveness 16
Authenticity 17
Keeping Our Feet on the Ground 18
The Hope of Seeking God 19
Prayer of Compassion 20
Mercy 21
For Children Who Beg on the Streets 22
Facing Life in Love 23
Calling on the Breath of God 24
The Desire of Stillness 25
A Surge of Hope for the Jobless 26
The Longing Gaze of God 27
Prayer of Longing 28
The Right to Be 29
Prayer to Live the Rule of God 30
Carrying the Vision of Love 31
Psalm 23 by a Seeker in Need of Comfort 32
Hospitality 34

The God Whom I Love is Here	35
The 8th Avenue Untouchable	36
Authentic Truth	38
Let Go and Be Still	39
The Naked, Sacred Vulnerability of Quiet Prayer	40
Speak to our Hearts of Strength and Courage	41
Voices That Challenge at the Food Pantry Café	42
Blessing of the Possible	46
Humility Defined	47
For Peace in a Land of Hell	48
Action with Hope	49
Blessing Prayer for Friends	50
God-Quest	51
In the Market for Balance and Perspective	52
The Metronome of Prayer	53
Letting Go	54
The Amazing Race	55
For the Way of Help That is Needed Soon	56
Invitation to the Feast of Life	57
3 Questions with a Soul Friend	58
Blessing of the 5 Senses	59
Prayer to the Ms. Jane Doe Within Me	60
Tending the Vineyard of the Earth	62
What to Do With Doubt and Worry	63
What Time is it?	64
For an End to Violent Attacks against Women	67

There's an Uprising of Hope	68
Spiritual Questions	69
Enwrapped by God	70
The Call to Listen	71
Strength Beyond the Rate of Unemployment	72
Mary's Canticle to a Daughter of God	74
The Urgent Need for Security and Peace	76
Simple words of Wisdom	77
Moving our Feet in Prayer	78
Prayer in the Struggle	79
Prayer of Psalm 139	80
Prayer for the Life of Longevity among the Poor	82
God and Money	84
Preaching	85
In the Silence	86
Soulful Listening to God	87
Magnificat of Gratitude	88
Generosity Driven by Compassion and Love	90
Blessing Prayer of Autumn	92
Blessing of the Breath of God	94
Bethlehem - House of Bread	95
A Christmas Wish List	96
About the Author	99

Prayer for a Dawning Hope

Holy One of Infinite Love,

your fragrance of grace wafts upon us

like the scent of fresh rain upon blooming earth.

As new life buds forth from the sacred soil,

nudge us to lean into the dark

with a waking heart and keen awareness

to your Spirit

breaking forth like morning dawn -

re-creating us anew in love once more.

May your blessing grow our hope

in the dawning of a new day,

a new season, a new moment. Amen.

God the Faithful One

Let us be mindful

that God is the Faithful One

who is calling us to a deeper life.

Let us continue to make room for God,

to prepare a space for God

in our hearts and in our lives.

The Recession of Worry That Won't Go Away

For all those receding more into worry, we pray.

For all those who waver

under the mounting carnage of crisis, we pray.

For all those who have lost their footing

in the job market, we pray.

For all of us wading through a recession, we pray.

We pray for hope, for relief,

for an iron will of strength,

and for courage.

Listen to your people O God,

for this we pray. Amen.

In the Image and Likeness

Each day

we are faced with the opportunity

to love as God loves.

Let us pay attention

to how we act and live

in the name of Love.

A Sacred Moment of Letting Go

Let go and breathe deeply of God.

Silence,

Solitude,

the rhythm of a contemplative day,

a sacred moment with God,

a grateful heart.

Catch your breath.

Breathe deeply.

All is gift.

The Longing Ache of God

No matter where we are

along our journey of faith,

or on our God-quest,

or in our searching for God,

it is God who invites us to life abundantly,

to a deeper life of love and grace.

Only God

can satisfy

the ache and longing in our hearts.

A Rainbow of Silence

The Silence of God

speaks a deeper connection beyond words.

> Silence that regenerates.
>
> Silence that affirms.
>
> Silence that loves.

We stand in awe of the Mystery,

in awe of watching a rainbow appear in the sky,

a symbol of God's covenant love.

We pray in gratitude for the reminder to love always.

Prayer of Attentiveness

O God,

help us to listen

with all our heart and

with all our soul.

May we pay attention

to Your Divine Presence

in all things,

and may the life we live

be a song of praise to You. Amen.

Authenticity

To be authentic,

to put our faith into action,

what we believe in our hearts,

what we profess with our lips,

how we serve with our hands and feet,

how we walk our talk,

requires an attentiveness

and awareness

of God's presence

within us,

between us,

and around us.

Keeping Our Feet on the Ground

Loving God of Heaven and Earth,

In the midst of crisis,

we are reminded more than ever

that our journey in this world is a pilgrimage to You,

and that we belong to You O God.

Help us keep our feet on the ground

and walk in the ways of justice.

May Your Spirit remind us to carry love

in the backpack of our hearts along the road of life.

Help us pay attention

to the earth, to nature, all of creation and humankind,

to our family, friends, loved ones and neighbors -

all tangible reminders of Your presence.

In our pilgrimage of life,

may we be seekers of the good in this world

and reach out to help others along the way.

Crisis or not,

may we always pay attention

to what really matters in life.

Hear us O God as we pray, Amen.

The Hope of Seeking God

As we seek God in hope

let us allow God

to find us in love.

Prayer of Compassion

God of Compassion

hold us in hope.

God of Compassion

call us to love.

God of Compassion

fill us with peace. Amen.

Mercy

God's mercy

is not about fairness

but about generosity.

For Children Who Beg on the Streets

Compassionate God,

We pray for children

who stand along the road and plead for food,

 hoping a passing truck

will toss a lifeline of nourishment.

Wrap your arms of Love around children

who suffer from the trauma and devastation

of natural disasters,

who beg for food on the streets,

who are victims of poorly managed governments.

May their hunger for survival

 be enfolded by endless rations

of food, clothing, shelter,

peace, and life abundantly.

Inspire your servants

to come to their aid quickly.

May we be your hands and feet of help

and your caring arms of love.

Hear us O God, for this we pray. Amen.

Facing Life in Love

We are cradled in love

by a God who knows

every fiber of our being.

So live a life of seeking God.

Live with a mentality

of God's generosity and God's love –

yesterday, today, and tomorrow.

So live a life of seeking God.

Calling on the Breath of God

Spirit of God,

Breathe on us peace,

Breathe through us healing,

Breathe in us courage,

Breathe over us hope,

Breathe below us strength,

Breathe above us mercy,

Breathe around us joy,

Breathe on us love,

Spirit of God,

we pray and breathe in gratitude. Amen.

The Desire of Stillness

Be still this day,

this moment

and go deeper into God.

A Surge of Hope for the Jobless

Compassionate God

You who fashion us for work,

You who call us to labor in the fields of humanity,

Hear the prayers of those who suffer from layoffs,

who struggle with unemployment,

who suffer from anxiety and worry

over the status of their job, their benefits,

their livelihood, their very existence.

Grant them courage and strength

to weather the storms of crisis.

Hold them in a community of support and care.

May a surge of hope

emerge from the depths of their stress.

Inspire them with a creative spirit

and a willing heart

to keep going in the land of labor.

Hear us O Holy One.

For this we pray, Amen.

The Longing Gaze of God

God paces at the window of our souls,

leaning forward, peering in,

seeking and longing for us.

God aches to be at one with us.

Prayer of Longing

Today God,

we long so much to see Your face,

to shake hands with the mountains,

to kiss the beautiful sky

and to walk Your sacred ground. Amen.

The Right to Be

I am a firm believer

that everyone

has the right

to be themselves.

Prayer to Live the Rule of God

Creator God,

Your rule is to love,

to love with all our heart and mind,

body, soul and being,

and to love each other

as we love our very self.

So just this day,

may we be rooted in love,

may we be rooted in You O God,

and may we embody and live

the rule of love for all people.

May we linger longer in love, in God,

just this day,

For our lives are compatible with You -

Abundant, Gracious and Loving One.

Let us be rooted in love, just this day. Amen.

Carrying the Vision of Love

What do we need to carry to God to prayer this day,

to widen our vision of love?

This no-greater-love,

this laying down of our lives kind of love,

this giving of ourselves for the sake of love,

for God's love;

this commandment to love

and to be with God in the world

through friendship,

this is the love we seek.

Psalm 23 by a Seeker in Need of Comfort

The Lord is my shepherd, I shall not want;

    but I do want Lord.

You let me rest in fields of green grass,

    yet the grass may turn brown.

You lead me to quiet pools of fresh water;

    but sometimes, the way may be rough.

You give me new strength because I am weak.

You guide me in the right paths, as you have promised.

If only I will follow; sometimes I may stumble and fall.

Even if I go through deepest darkness,

    I will not be afraid, for you are with me.

        But I am afraid.

Your shepherd's rod and staff protect me.

You prepare a banquet for me,

    where all my enemies can see me;

        sometimes I refuse the invitation.

Still, you welcome me as an honored guest

    and fill my cup to the brim.

I know that your goodness and love

    will be with me all my life

        and your house will be my home

        as long as I live.

Still, I need to hear those words

    of goodness and comfort once more. Amen.

Adaptation of Psalm 23 originally written in 1985

Hospitality

We are called

to provide a hospitality of love

that empowers others

to be their best, genuine self

fully alive in God.

The God Whom I Love is Here

Listen,

    the God whom I love is here,

    singing in the birds.

Listen,

    the God whom I love is waiting,

    waiting for my soul to catch up

    to the world of spiritual beauty and holiness.

Listen,

    the God whom I love is here,

    in the silent places of my heart.

Listen…

    in the silent places.

Listen,

    the God whom I love is present,

    in the silent places.

Listen.

The 8th Avenue Untouchable

I never saw your face.

But I knew you were in pain

quietly suffering

amidst the din of New York City chaos.

Your hands – broken and bruised

as you held a cup

begging for some change,

pleading for something called dignity.

Only a cardboard sign identified you:

> *Homeless Vet, Dying of AIDS*
> *Please Help! Thank you*

You sat

head between your knees,

your arms crossed,

daring to hold that damn plastic cup

out into the busy-ness,

hoping for relief,

praying for someone or something

to disturb your silent hell.

I never saw your face.

Somehow,

your presence grabbed my heart,

in a fleeting moment

I wanted to stop

and to touch you,

to look into your eyes.

Instead of giving you money,

I wanted to give you compassion,

a sense of human dignity,

a sense of self-worth,

a sense of love.

But I kept on walking....

And, I never saw your face.

New York, June, 1990

Authentic Truth

We have to live

the truth of our faith

in order to be authentic.

Anything less

is not an option.

Let Go and Be Still

Loving God,

You call us to be here and to be still.

Help us to let go -

to let go of the fears, the worries,

the endless tasks racing through our minds.

Help us to let God -

to let you O God speak to us

in the mountains of our hearts.

Let our hearts be one with You O God -

mountain and majesty.

May You soften our resistance.

Call us once more to be here and to be still. Amen.

The Naked, Sacred Vulnerability of Quiet Prayer

Quiet is the threshold moment

of moving from a naked vulnerability

to a sacred love with God.

We must be willing to take the risk

 to sit in the quiet and

believe that God knows us full well,

where everything about us is exposed.

We are naked before God,

and we are called to trust

that this place of quiet is a safe place

of sacred, holy love with God.

Quiet is intimate prayer at its best.

Where is that place of quiet for you?

Where do you find moments

    of stillness and quiet in your day?

Go there, and go there often with God.

Speak to our Hearts of Strength and Courage

O Great Spirit,

Voice of God

speak to our hearts once again.

We remember the mountainside stream,

waters stirring within,

awashed with the sounds,

of Your Presence,

of Your Wisdom,

of Your Understanding.

Holy One, speak to our hearts once again.

Grant us strength and courage once more. Amen.

Voices That Challenge at the Food Pantry Café

"It's 11:35,

partly cloudy today,

hazy, hot and humid,

high of 94 degrees...."

So says the voice of the oldies station DJ

in the Washington area.

Voices that challenge....

Three drawers of files,

three days of filing,

a file-by-pile method.

The radio

is the voice I hear

as I tear

perforated computer edges

amidst WIC forms and CSFP papers.

The cadence of the supervisor

echoes metronomically,

"Throw out those beyond June, 1991.

Each person applies every six months."

Every six months

for aid –

food for the elderly,

food for women –

expecting life,

giving life,

feeding life.

Caution

is the voice I hear

as I throw away the first few pages.

Detachment comes later.

"These are peoples' lives you're throwing away"

is the voice I hear inside.

I sound like the government.

Wishful thinking, huh?

I volunteered for this job

because papers don't talk back to you.

They don't have an attitude.

I don't have to relate

to other voices

that challenge,

that question,

that scream

in anger and frustration.

Voices that challenge….

Who are those voices on file, A-Z?

Two drawers for the elderly

over 60 no doubt.

One drawer for women and children.

Names like

Thurmalita, Juanita,

Nathaniel, Napoleon;

Johnson, Brown, Mayo.

Birthdays like

1896, 1902, 1913,

1989, 1994.

Who are these voices?

Folks in the neighborhood

who stumble pushing a grocery cart,

stumble for bread,

stumble with a sauntering limp,

coming to fill their baskets:

all brought to you by the AFDC.

Voices that challenge....

Can I hear their voices on those pages?

Can I see their faces?

Do I dare listen?

Inspired by volunteer work at Sojourners Food Pantry – Washington, DC – June 1994
WIC = Women, Infants & Children
CSFP = Commodity Supplemental Food Program
AFDC = Aid to Families with Dependent Children

Blessing of the Possible

Blessed are we

who believe

in the possibility of God.

Humility Defined

Some people think

that to be humble means

you lie down and be a doormat

for people to walk all over you.

That's not being humble;

that's being dysfunctional.

To be humble is to be grounded

in the truth of who you are.

Humility

is about being rooted

in genuine honesty

and authenticity.

Humility

is about integrity.

For Peace in a Land of Hell

Let us pray fervently for those

who find themselves immersed in the violence of hell,

a hell that is not their own choosing.

For all those

who are isolated in swampy jungles,

who live on shortages of food, fuel and electricity,

who take shelter in bullet-ridden homes,

who pray in shrapnel-pitted temples;

for those who live with the constant fear

of those wearing vests of suicide bombs,

who live under the curfew of night

and in the terror of disappearances and killings.

May this prison island of hell be transformed quickly

into a land of tranquility with lasting ethnic harmony.

May a labyrinth of peace

be the only checkpoint of security.

Most of all, may the fighting end soon and very soon.

We hurry our prayer to you O God.

Hear us as we pray, Amen.

Action with Hope

Every day,

do something

to move you out the door

toward something else

in attitude, thoughts, or actions.

Make small steps toward hope.

Blessing Prayer for Friends

Blessed are You, God of all creation

For You give us the gift of friendship.

We remember and we give You thanks and praise.

May Your Spirit empower us courageously with hope

when our hearts are troubled,

touch us gently with peace

when we walk our separate paths,

and caress us softly with grace

when we encounter pain and suffering along the way;

so that our hearts may rejoice

as we continue to act justly, to love tenderly,

and to walk humbly with You, O God.

Blessed are You, loving and faithful God

For You call us friends.

You call us to love one another,

to be friend to one another,

to lay down our lives for each other.

We give You thanks,

and so we cry from the depths of our being: YES!

For there is no greater love than this. Amen.

God-Quest

What is your intention when you go to worship?

What is your intention when you go to pray?

What is your intention when you go to the mountains?

What are you looking for?

What do you seek?

How do you wait?

How do you listen?

In the Market for Balance and Perspective

Creator God,

whose love and goodness

are not measured in financial terms,

we thank you for the gift of life

and for the constant reminder

that there is more to life than mere survival.

Hear us as we pray:

The reality is that we live in a culture

where money and economics matter.

Help us keep perspective

as we struggle to understand

and work our way through a financial crisis.

Help us walk the way of justice

in a world often controlled by greed.

Help us live in the balance,

centered in Your love O God.

This we pray:

for a life of perspective, balance and justice.

Hear us O God. Amen.

The Metronome of Prayer

Listen to your heart

for there you will find

the pulse of your soul

beating in harmony with God.

Letting Go

Let go.

Let go of the fears.

Let God.

Let God speak to you

    in the mountains of your heart.

Let your heart be one with God

    in the mountains.

Let God soften the resistance.

Be here and be still.

The Amazing Race

Life is a journey
> of living fully in every moment,
>> holding nothing back,
>>> and giving our all.

For the Way of Help That is Needed Soon

We pray for all people who are burdened

by the weight of the recessionary economy;

For those who stand in an unemployment line;

For those buried under the mound of debt,

For those who stand on the edge of foreclosure,

and for those who have fallen

into the abyss of bankruptcy.

May anchors of hope

be cast in deep waters of strength.

May life lines of stability

be thrown with the might of relief.

May the rescue of empowerment

be launched with the thrusters of determination.

And may help for all

be on the way soon and very soon.

For this we pray

in the name of the God

of goodness, love and peace.

Hear us O God. Amen.

Invitation to the Feast of Life

This day,

we are called to dine with God,

for God invites us

to the great feast of life,

this lavish feast

of inclusive, generous love.

How will we RSVP?

3 Questions with a Soul Friend

1) What was the best part of your day?

2) What was the hardest part?

3) Where did you see God this day?

                    Thanks be to God. Amen.

Blessing of the 5 Senses

May you walk this day

with a mindfulness of God

all around you and within.

For God is beneath the ground of your feet.

God is within the grasp of your touch.

The fragrance of God lingers in the air under your nose.

The sound of God pulsates at the drum of your ear lobe.

God's taste of love is placed upon your lips.

God is within your vision

this moment, this day, every day of your life.

May you walk this day with a mindfulness of God. Amen.

Prayer to the Ms. Jane Doe Within Me

It was a Sunday afternoon, the Laundro-mat,

as I waited for the final rinse,

she sat quietly in a chair next to me,

puffing slowly on a cigarette,

listening to God-only-knows what

through her headphones.

Her arms were crossed in front;

her hands tightly clenching an ashtray.

On her face,

she wore the expression

of a lifeless, empty womb.

Her head never turned,

and her eyes didn't wander.

The door was shut

and the windows locked.

I couldn't even get close enough

to say "hello," or "how are you?"

much less knock

to see if anybody was home.

I don't think I would recognize

this woman if I sat next to her again.

Or would I?

Tending the Vineyard of the Earth

God has entrusted us with the vineyard of the earth,

the vineyard of other people's heart and soul.

We are called to be responsible stewards,

not absentee landlords or half-hearted tenants.

We are called to be a light of hope for our world,

to be a witness of love in the face of a violent society,

to be committed to right relationships,

to be willing to labor with all our being

in the vineyard with God,

to give our lives in an act of love

that is life-giving for ourselves and for others.

What to Do With Doubt and Worry

Doubts and worries are part of living

and they can be a way

to deepen our longing for God,

when we pray at the honest depth of our needs,

when we pray our vulnerability with God.

Bring your doubts and worries to that sacred space.

What Time is it?

What time is it?

A simple question;

a not-so-easy answer.

Time:

we keep it;

we manage it;

we save it;

we measure it;

we waste it;

we lose it.

Chronological time –

the measure of marking when we work,

when we play,

when we pray,

when we sleep,

and when we rest.

Chronos – the span of linear time;

a tool to measure the order of our lives.

Enter God's time – *Kairos* –

a decisive point in time;

where time becomes timeless;

where life slows down;

moments when we pray,

time seems endless;

time enters a quiet solitude;

time becomes gratitude,

an amazing act of beauty.

A decisive point in time –

God's in-breaking moments into our lives.

God's time – the present moment.

What time is it in your life?

In what ways are you paying attention

to the moments of God's time, *Kairos*,

breaking in to your calendars,

your Day-Timer,

your schedule?

How is the watch of your life set to God's time?

How is the calendar of your heart

 synchronized to God's love?

In what ways is the metronome of your faith

beating to the rhythm of God's music?

God's justice?

God's peace?

What time is it for you?

For an End to Violent Attacks against Women

Creator God,

You who made women and men

in Your image and likeness,

hear the prayers of those

who suffer violent attacks

because of their gender.

Embrace them with the balm of healing.

Protect them with a shield

of love, strength and courage.

May there be an end to violent attacks

against women and young girls throughout our world.

Inspire all of us to stand up

and defend the human rights of all people,

especially the most vulnerable.

For this we pray, Amen.

Written for the women and girls of Afghanistan

There's an Uprising of Hope

Rise up,

Rise up all people,

Speak out,

Speak out in courage,

Sisters and brothers,

Join in the stirring,

There's an uprising of hope all people,

We're an uprising of hope.

Spiritual Questions

What do you want?

What is at the heart of the matter for you?

What is at the depth of your soul?

Are you willing to be changed?

Are you willing to see and to live

    with a divine perspective for one another?

Enwrapped by God

At a very chaotic moment in my life,

I asked you O God, to be present with me…

to help me keep things in perspective…..

(Did I really know what I was asking for?)

As silence flooded my heart,

I felt your Spirit encircle and enwrap me;

You surrounded me like a warm, quilted blanket,

and held me close to you

as a mother holds a child in her arms.

In that moment of stillness,

all my fears melted away;

the stress of life vanished,

and nothing else seemed to matter.

My only focus was being in Your Presence,

and feeling rooted, secure, safe, loved,

protected, centered, balanced, nurtured, unafraid.

Oh, so loved. Oh, so surprised.

Thank you God

for overwhelming me with Your Love. Amen.

From a Peruvian travel journal, April 1990

The Call to Listen

O Word of God,

You are near to us

and deep in our hearts.

Help us pay attention

and lean in closer to You,

this day,

this moment,

this time of now. Amen.

Strength Beyond the Rate of Unemployment

Creator God,

You who worked to form the universe,

You who labored to bring forth the earth into being,

You who fashioned humanity

    in Your image and likeness,

hear the prayers of those

who find themselves unemployed for a long time,

who have recently lost a job,

who are concerned about losing their job in the future.

Worry is on the mind of many.

Anxiety is the source of stress.

In a culture governed by economics,

in a time of high energy prices,

a housing slump, and faltering market,

may Your Spirit breathe a gentle calm

over anxious hearts and worried minds.

Grant us strength to endure the hard times,

courage to believe

in the determination of the human spirit;

give us a vision of creativity and imagination,

and hope in a life beyond financial survival.

Hear us O God. Amen.

Mary's Canticle to a Daughter of God

The unknown….
    not an easy journey.
Trust in the Spirit
    hovering over you
    and within.
The Incarnation stirs within you,
    groaning and laboring
    to give you birth,
    to call you to love,
    a love so deep-hearted
    in the whole of your being;
    a birthing of Christ
    in you
    for others.
You are blessed
    among women and men
    and children and grandparents.
Desire
    to seek
    the face of the living God.

Listen to that Voice
>   deep within you.

Christ is coming,
>   in fact,
>   already here.

Look.
>   Listen.
>   >   Believe.

Rejoice.
>   Be patient.
>   >   Persevere.

Trust and love
>   above all else.

The Urgent Need for Security and Peace

In the midst of violence and escalating terrorist threats,
> we pray.

In the midst of religious extremism, we pray.

In the midst of suicide bombers, we pray.

We pray for an end to hatred
> among nations and religions.

We pray for a greater strength in security.

We pray for an empowerment of local people
> to stand firm.

We pray for an understanding toward peace
> and tolerance of one another.

Most of all, we pray that the terror of fear
> be replaced by the assurance of hope.

May harmony, peace, and tolerance of diversity
> be a lasting source of protection for all people.

Hear us O God,

the ONE GOD
> of many religions, faith and spiritual traditions.

For this we pray, Amen.

Simple words of Wisdom

Smile with peace.

Desire only God.

Explore the questions.

Worry not.

Moving our Feet in Prayer

"When you pray, move your feet."
African Proverb

Compassionate God,

You who hear the cry of the poor,

Hear the cries of those

who hunger for food and life throughout our world:

those in urban and farm areas who suffer

    from drought, famine, political instability,

        and economic disaster.

Merciful God,

You who call all your followers to action,

Move our feet toward justice,

Give us strength to walk our talk with integrity,

Listen to our plea, and

Guide our feet in the ways of peace, justice and love. Amen.

Prayer in the Struggle

Oh God,

there are many struggles in our lives right now.

Let us not struggle this night. Amen.

Prayer of Psalm 139

O God, you have searched me, you have found me,
    and you know me.
You know when I sit and when I stand.
You know when I succeed and when I fail.
You are familiar with all my ways.
You know my thoughts even before I think them.
And even before I speak,
    you know what I will say, O God.

You are behind me and before me, and
    you have laid your hand up on me.
Such knowledge is too wonderful for me.
O God, you are awesome.

Where can I go from your Spirit?
Where can I run from your presence?
If I climb the Rocky Mountains or
    travel from Boston to Seattle,
you are there.

If I sail around the world or stay in my back yard,

    even there, you will be with me and guide me.

If I think the darkness can hide me, I am wrong.

For the darkness is like the day to you.

For you created me O God,

And I praise you because

    I am fearfully and wonderfully made.

All your works are wonderful, and I know that full well.

Even before I was made in that secret place O God,

    you knew all my days before one of them began.

To me, you are like a precious jewel.

I have found a treasure.

Search me, O God, and know my heart.

Test me O God, and know my anxious thoughts.

See if there is any offensive way in me, and get rid of it.

And lead me in the way everlasting. Amen.

Adaptation of Psalm 139 originally written in 1986

Prayer for the Life of Longevity among the Poor

On this day

Let us pray for those who celebrate birthdays

    of longevity,

For those who celebrate the struggle for freedom,

For those who work tirelessly for the rights of the poor,

For those who peacefully fight against oppression.

Let us pray for those still gripped by poverty,

Let us pray for those still imprisoned by illiteracy,

Let us pray for those still suffering from AIDS,

Let us pray for those still afflicted by racism.

May we run with flags of peace

    around the jails of injustice.

May we lay roads of education

    to the doorsteps of the unskilled.

May flowers of healing be the balm for the sick.

May bowls of tolerance

    be the nourishment for the discriminated.

May all of us share

the wealth of our resources,

so that poverty may be conquered

one village at a time.

Hear us O God, we pray, Amen.

In honor of Nelson Mandela's 90th Birthday – July 18, 2008

God and Money

We do not bear the mark of a dollar bill,

    a stock certificate

    or a bank account

on our hearts,

but the very imprint of God.

We bear the inscription of God

    in our souls.

How we are rooted in God,

how live our lives

    regardless of our financial situation,

is the essential matter.

Preaching

Preach the Gospel and the stuff of your life.

Hopefully the two are closely related.

No, the two must be intimately connected.

In the Silence

In the Silence, name me O God,

In the Silence, heal me O God,

In the Silence, free me O God,

In the Silence, save me O God,

In the Silence, name me O God,

In the Silence, claim me O God,

In the Silence, teach me O God,

In the Silence, tame me O God.

Soulful Listening to God

Where do you go

    to commune more deeply with God?

Where do you go

    to hear the still small voice of your soul?

How do you pay attention to God

    who journeys with you in the midst of your seeking?

Go there as often as you can.

Magnificat of Gratitude

My soul proclaims your lavishness O God,

because you have poured out your love abundantly,

energetically, and with wild abandon.

In the stillness and deep-down solitude of being,

I speak of my passion for you, O God.

Music fills my being,

for I hear flashes of your melody ringing in my soul,

and echoes of the melodies of life

teeming amidst an orchestra of creation:

mountain, forest, pine tree, pond,

beaver, geese, dragonfly,

and a chorus of bullfrogs.

Within the depths of my being,

I am consumed by awe and reverence,

transformed into a vessel of sacred silence.

In this pottery of human frailty, I am filled with joy,

a joy that can only be contained

by breath-taking wonder.

My heart overflows with gratitude and praise.

I breathe deeply and walk at the speed of life.

I will sing and make music to my God forever more.

Alleluia. Amen.

Inspired by Luke 1:47-55

Generosity Driven by Compassion and Love

Blessed are You

Compassionate God,

You who inspire others to action,

who give beyond their measure

even during challenging economic times.

Blessed are You

Steadfast God,

You who encourage scientists and doctors

to press forward in medical research.

Blessed are You

Gentle God,

You who enfold children in love,

and sit with relatives at the bedside of their sick children.

For the tireless efforts of your caring servants,

for their generous hearts and determined spirits,

We give you thanks Abundant God.

May their generosity continue to be driven

 by love and compassion.

May others be so inspired to do the same.

With a grateful spirit in the name of love,

this we pray, Amen.

In honor of Jerry Lewis and the MDA Telethon

Blessing Prayer of Autumn

Wind of Heaven,

May we listen to your Spirit

    moving in the air of Autumn:

A season of transition, a season of change;

A season of harvest, a bounty of goodness;

A season of mystery, of dying and letting go;

A season of trust, of new life being promised again.

May we take time to find moments of quiet in our life.

May we be inspired to pay closer attention.

Spirit of the Earth,

May beauty emerge within us.

May the vivid colors of our gifts come into view.

May the branches of our souls

    reveal our essential core of goodness.

O Great Spirit of Autumn,

Grant us courage

    to live your wisdom and witness your beauty.

May we fall into the mystery and step forward in trust.

May we discover moments of rest

    and a harvest of nourishment.

Great Spirit of Autumn,

Wind of Heaven,

Spirit of the Earth,

Thank you for the blessing of this day. Amen.

Blessing of the Breath of God

May the Breath of God blow through our being.

May the Spirit of God breathe a promise of dawn.

May the Breath of God stir a new story within us.

May the Spirit of God

    be the wind of hope under our feet.

May the Breath of God fill us with peace. Amen.

Bethlehem - House of Bread

This is the time when God comes to us

as a child and in bread;

when the divine star of love

radiates hope;

when the human face of God

is made flesh in vulnerability.

May you follow

this radiant Star of Light

with a twinkle of wonder

and a glowing ember of courage,

on the trail of being,

living on the edge of peace,

sharing bread with sojourners

on the road to the House of Bread.

A Christmas Wish List

What do you want for Christmas?

This is a common question

parents ask their children

as the holiday time approaches.

Even among adults,

there is a child-like wonder in making a wish list –

things we hope to receive at Christmas time.

Here is my Christmas wish list:
- A blanket of peace covering the world
- Food and shelter for every homeless person
- A coat of justice for the vulnerable
- Compassion for those who walk alone
- Inspiration for those wearied by indifference
- Hope for those in the trenches of making a difference in the world

What do you want for Christmas?

What is the desire of your heart?

For what do you long?

For what do you wish?

May all your hopes and prayers become possible.

About the Author

Over the past 25 years, Denise Pyles has been a Christian pastoral minister specializing in preaching, leading worship services and directing music. She is a former nun, holds a Masters of Divinity degree, and is a musician and composer of three recordings of original music. Currently, she is a project manager and a licensed wedding official. Originally from Louisville, KY, she now lives in Seattle, WA where she spends her time living the adventure of life wholeheartedly. This is her second book.

www.ingramcontent.com/pod-product-compliance
Lightning Source LLC
Chambersburg PA
CBHW051955290426
44110CB00015B/2247